W9-AOM-085

Everything You Need to Know About

Volunteering

One person can make a difference in the world!
Volunteering is a way to act on issues that you care about.

Everything You Need to Know About

Volunteering

Laura Weeldreyer

The Rosen Publishing Group, Inc.
New York

To Bryna and Harvey Fireside, for your many years of volunteer service and your tireless commitment to peace and justice.

Published in 2001 by The Rosen Publishing Group, Inc.
29 East 21st Street, New York, NY 10010

First Edition

Library of Congress Cataloging-in-Publication Data

Weeldreyer, Laura
  Everything you need to know about volunteering/ by Laura
Weeldreyer.—1st ed.
      p. cm. — (The need to know library)
Includes bibliographical references and index.
  ISBN 0-8239-3220-6 (lib. bdg. : alk. paper)
  1. Voluntarism—United States—Juvenile literature. 2. Young volunteers—United States—Juvenile literature. I. Title. II. Series.
  HN90.V64.W4 2001
  361.3'7'0973—dv21

                                                    00-008735

Manufactured in the United States of America

Contents

Introduction

Do you live in a city or town where homelessness is a problem? Do you have a family member or a friend who suffers from an illness and needs help? Have you or anyone you know survived a disaster like a fire or a tornado? Have you ever seen a story on television or in the newspaper that touched you and made you wonder how you could help? That feeling is the spirit of volunteering: the desire to help others, to take a stand on an issue, to make a difference in the world.

Volunteering is a way to act on issues you care about. You may think, "I'm just one person. What can I possibly do?" You would be surprised: You can do a lot! Your efforts can improve people's lives, change the outcome of events, and shape the future for the better. It is one sure way of experiencing how you, one individual, can make a difference in the world. You will be filled with the confidence and knowledge that you can do something important. Volunteering is a win-win proposition.

As a teen volunteer, you will have a lot of company. Did you know that six out of ten American teens volunteer? In raw numbers, that translates to 13.3 million teens giving over 2.4 billion hours of volunteer service each year. More than two-thirds of those hours are spent in formal volunteer commitments, like working with a nonprofit organization, and a little under a third of those hours go to informal volunteer commitments, like helping an elderly neighbor. It would take more than one million employees to do all this work. Think of the money teens are saving the nonprofit organizations that do valuable work for our communities.

Everyone has something to give as a volunteer. You can use your spare time and special talents to make a difference in the world.

Chapter One | Things to Consider

Your interests are unique to you, as are your reasons for volunteering. Everyone has something to give, whether it's a special talent or simply the gift of time. Energy, enthusiasm, and dependability are usually the primary requirements for a volunteer. Think about what you care about and what you like to do. If you like animals, you could consider volunteering at the local animal shelter. If you enjoy children, you could volunteer in the children's ward at a hospital. If you are well organized, offer your services to help run a special event, like a walk-a-thon. If it's money you like, you could help run a fund-raiser for a nonprofit organization. If you care about the environment and you are artistic, you could make signs for your community, encouraging citizens to recycle. In chapter 2 you will have the opportunity to conduct a self-assessment test to help you figure out what issues are most important to you and what kind of volunteer work best fits your talents.

Volunteering: A Rewarding Way to Spend Your Time

The rewards from volunteering are many. Not only will you help others and perform a valuable service, you will learn about issues or organizations that interest you, gain potential job-related experience (volunteering looks great on a résumé or college application), meet interesting people, and have fun.

Volunteering also gives you perspective on life, which may be the most valuable reward in the long run. Volunteering gives you the opportunity to learn about aspects of life that you may never personally experience. You may never be homeless, but volunteering at a homeless shelter or a soup kitchen gives you the rare opportunity to get a glimpse into lives that are different from your own.

Be realistic about how much you can give

It's important to remember that volunteering is a serious commitment and you must consider some things before you jump into a project. You should assess your workload

In a 1996 survey, when asked why they volunteer, teens listed many personal reasons, including:

- Feeling of compassion toward people in need

- Feeling that you can contribute to a cause that is important to you

- Belief that if you help others, others will help you

- Belief that volunteering is important to people you respect (like parents, teachers, religious leaders)

- Learn to relate to others who are different from you

- Develop leadership skills

- Become more patient

- Gain a better understanding of good citizenship

- Get a chance to learn about various careers

- Gain experience that can help in school and lead to college admission and college scholarships as well as future careers

Volunteering at a soup kitchen can give you a perspective on lives that are different from your own.

and whether you have enough time to take on a volunteer activity, especially given the fact that you will not be paid for your work. If you already have a job along with schoolwork, be realistic about your time constraints.

There can be a certain amount of stress in volunteering. Caring for others can put you under pressure, and—depending on the kind of work you decide upon—you may be exposed to some pretty sobering stuff. Think about how much you can handle without feeling emotionally exhausted. Working with people who are ill or serving meals in a soup kitchen, for example, may expose you to people and situations you have never dealt with before. Be prepared to handle new people and new situations with maturity. There is always a need for volunteers to take on more work or volunteer more of their time. Don't feel compelled or pressured to take on more than you can comfortably handle.

Can You Be Required to Volunteer?

More and more young people are being required to volunteer. In fact, if you go to school in Maryland or in Atlanta, Georgia, you will be required to volunteer a certain number of hours in order to graduate from high school. Many school districts are adopting this policy, which is called service learning or community service. Many believe that volunteer work is an essential part of education. Even colleges and universities are getting into the act and requiring the same sorts of activities—sometimes called communiversity hours— in order to get a college diploma.

Making an Impact

You never know what the future might hold. And you never know how your volunteer services, enthusiasm, and energy today may change the outcome of tomorrow. Volunteering might lead you to your future career, introduce you to life-long friends, or teach you something that you would have never learned otherwise. Volunteering helps ensure that the future will be a better place. How can you resist being part of a movement to make this world a kinder, safer, cleaner, and more just home for the six billion people who live here?

Chapter Two

Causes to Care About

There are plenty of causes and organizations in need of volunteers. The choice of which one to donate your time to is all up to you. So take the time to think through your values and concerns about the world. Have you ever seen the bumper sticker that says, "Think globally, act locally"? Think big about the world but find a way to impact it right in your own home-town. You may want to choose an issue that "hits close to home." In other words, you may feel most strongly about an issue that affects your community, your family, or your school. It could be worth your time to read the newspaper and watch the local news for a while to get an idea about pressing needs in your community.

No one can deny that there are many problems to be solved on this planet. Here are some examples of causes that rely on the generosity of volunteers like you.

Homelessness and Shelter

No one knows exactly how many people are homeless in the United States. Experts put the number somewhere between 250,000 and 600,000. However, everyone agrees that the problem of homelessness is growing in alarming ways. More and more families with small children are becoming homeless. Homeless children are deprived of the stability necessary for a comfortable childhood. They suffer from improper nutrition, they do not receive an adequate education, and they are often forced to witness drug abuse, crime, and the breakup of their families.

If you live in or near a city, you are most likely near at least one homeless shelter that serves meals and provides beds and other services to homeless people. Most shelters welcome volunteers and will have a variety of ways in which you can get involved. Volunteers do everything from preparing and serving meals and helping to raise money to working in the business office and assisting the clients of the shelter with personal tasks.

Hunger and Poverty

Being hungry is different from suffering from hunger. Suffering from hunger is not only about missing meals on a constant basis, it is not knowing where the next meal is coming from, or if it will come at all. According to the Second Harvest National Food Banks Network, 20 million people suffer from hunger at least a few

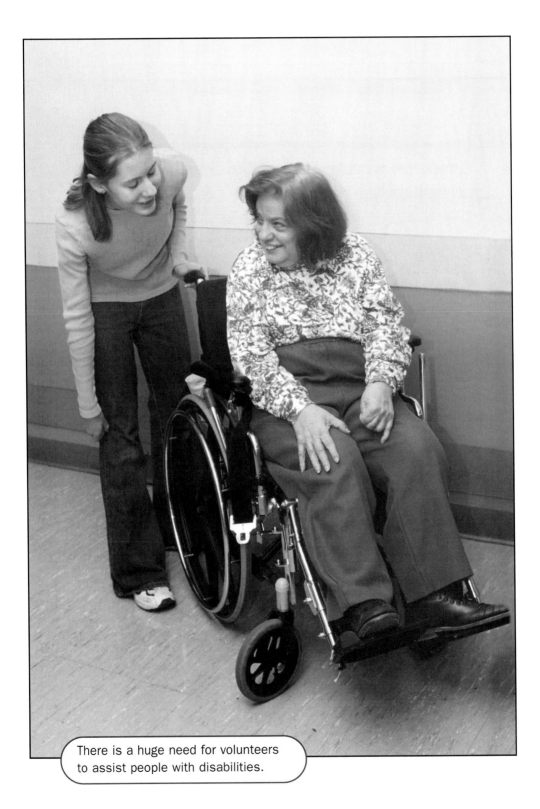

There is a huge need for volunteers to assist people with disabilities.

times each month. Many of these people are children. One out of every five children in this country lives in poverty and cannot consistently get proper nutrition.

Volunteers can get involved in fighting against hunger through soup kitchens or food pantries. You could help collect, prepare, and serve food. You can also help raise people's consciousness about hunger in your community by helping churches or schools organize food drives to collect canned goods.

There are also many agencies that serve the poor. Look in the phone book for the locations of organizations like Goodwill and the Salvation Army. You can help them solicit donations for the needy or organize a clothing drive in your community.

There are local chapters of Habitat for Humanity all over the United States (and the world) that build houses in poor communities and make home ownership a reality for many families who would otherwise never have one. You can check the Web site for the Habitat office closest to your community. There are often organized days and weeks of building during which volunteers can participate in all aspects of building a house.

Health and Disabilities

According to the National Organization on Disability, over 54 million men, women, and children in America have disabilities. Twenty-one million people are deaf or hearing impaired, 3 million are severely vision impaired, 120,000 are totally blind, 1.4 million people use wheelchairs, and 7 million people are mentally retarded. There are millions of others who suffer from chronic and debilitating illnesses each year. There is a huge need for people to assist the many individuals who are impaired in some way.

There are many organizations that help people with these various disabilities or diseases and depend on volunteers for fund-raising, help with special events, and assistance in serving patients. Maybe someone in your family has had cancer or you know someone who has leukemia. Maybe you have always wanted to learn how to read braille and are interested in helping the blind. Whatever your connection, there are many opportunities for volunteer service with or for people coping with illness. You could volunteer in a hospital, reading to patients, working with children, or even assisting nurses. Check out local candy-striper programs, which can provide you with real medical experience in hospitals and are ideal for teens who might be interested in a medical career.

Children

Children of all races, all religions, and all backgrounds are suffering throughout the United States from degrading situations like neglect, homelessness, and physical and emotional abuse. Children are the fastest growing segment of the homeless population. According to the Child Welfare League of America, child abuse is on the rise and the number of deaths from abuse has grown dramatically. These abused, hungry, hurt children are our future. This is a national crisis that deserves much attention.

There are many organizations that serve children and rely on volunteer help. Look in your phone book for local recreation centers or Boys and Girls Clubs, where you can tutor children, organize games or sports teams, or lead an arts and crafts lesson.

Children in foster care or children who are homeless often have to move frequently. Sometimes, children in foster care don't have access to a nice bag or suitcase in which to pack their clothes and belongings. Many teens around the country have organized very successful volunteer projects to collect suitcases for foster children through schools, churches, and community centers. This is a great example of teens wanting to make a difference in the lives of children.

The Elderly

The American Association of Retired Persons (AARP) estimates that there are more than 30 million people sixty-five and older in the United States. Many of these people volunteer regularly, but there is also a need for

There are many opportunities available to volunteer with elderly people.

younger volunteers to help those elderly people who are not as active and need help with daily tasks. Depression is a major issue for the elderly. Poverty also affects many older people who have no income but have high medical costs. Various organizations and even local homes for the elderly provide many opportunities to volunteer with aged people.

Nursing homes, hospitals, and assisted living communities are places where you can volunteer your time. These places happily welcome young people to assist with meals and recreational activities. You can read to residents, play games, or simply spend time with them. Maybe you have elderly neighbors who could use your help in running errands, shopping, home maintenance, and yard work.

Nature and the Environment

Pollutants, garbage, and chemicals are taking their toll on the land, the sea, and the air. According to the Environmental Action Foundation, the United States produces more than a ton of hazardous waste per person per year. This waste is poisoning the water supplies that many Americans depend on for their drinking water. Air pollution has become a major problem and over 110 million Americans live in areas with harmful levels of air pollutants. Unfortunately, we are destroying a major weapon that fights against air pollution—trees. According to the American Forestry Association, in the average American city, for every four trees that die or are removed, only one new tree is planted. At least 27 million acres of the rain forest are lost each year to land clearing and deforestation efforts, killing many important plant and animal species. Recycling and cutting down on consumption are keys to protecting the environment. Currently, the United States only recycles just over ten percent of its garbage.

Do you live near a state park? Many state parks have volunteer programs that look for people to build and maintain trails; lead educational programs, tours, and hikes; and develop activities and events for the park. Contact a state park near you and ask about volunteer opportunities. Some city parks have similar programs. Check

21

Julia Butterfly Hill—the Tree Woman

After surviving a terrible car accident, Julia Butterfly Hill felt the need to make a difference in the world. As fate would have it, in 1997, about one year after her accident, Hill ended up in a redwood forest, the Headwaters Forest in northern California, at a protest held by Earth First. The organization was protesting the systematic destruction of some of the world's oldest and largest trees—the giant redwoods. Hill was moved into action. "I knew I had to do something," she told *Blue* magazine. "I had to do something to help stop the destruction. I found out they needed someone to sit in Luna."

Luna is a redwood tree whose history reaches back some 1,000 years. Earth First found that an effective way to help save the trees was to have people sit in them. With people in the trees, the lumber company is unable to cut them down. Earth First had planned to make their point by having people sit in trees for two weeks. But when Hill sat in Luna, she decided she had found her mission.

Hill decided that she would not touch the ground again until she was guaranteed that Luna would not be cut down. With a dedicated ground crew and her profound determination, Hill tree-sat for two years and eight days—the longest period of time anyone has ever done such a thing. She lived on a small platform nestled in the branches of Luna, 180 feet above the ground, and got her exercise by climbing up and down the tree several times

a day. She survived harsh storms, many strong attempts by the Pacific Lumber Company—the company who owned the land—to bring her down, and loads of self-doubt. But all of those hardships served only to strengthen her determination. And on December 18, 1999, she was victorious. She reached an agreement with the company in which they agreed to protect Luna and trees on the 2.9 acres surrounding it in exchange for $50,000.

Hill now spends her time speaking out about environmental issues and has written a book entitled *The Legacy of Luna: The Story of a Tree, a Woman, and the Struggle to Save the Redwoods* (Harper San Francisco, 2000). Julia Butterfly Hill is just one example of what a difference one person's determination and dedication can make.

your local phone book for the parks department to get more information.

If you are interested in environmental issues like pollution, recycling, and the preservation of natural resources, check out the Sierra Club, Earth First, or another of the many environmental groups available to you. Most have chapters around the country. Neighborhood centers, churches, and schools are also places to look into that may have projects that help the environment, such as recycling drives or trash pick-up days.

Arts and Culture

Funding for cultural and art institutions has been greatly reduced in recent years, and these institutions are more dependent on volunteers than ever before. Museums, theaters, and symphonies are always looking for volunteers and often give you a chance to see plays, concerts, or exhibits for free. You can usher for a theater or work in the box office, become a docent (trained tour guide) for a museum, or pass out programs at concerts.

Literacy

According to the Basic Council for Effective Literacy, approximately 27 million adults over the age of seventeen—one out of every five adults—cannot read or write. That's 27 million adults who cannot read a newspaper headline, a medicine bottle, or a job application. Another 47 million are only minimally literate. Many people who cannot read often cannot find work. Illiteracy and a lack of education are closely connected with other societal problems, such as unemployment, homelessness, alcohol and drug abuse, and crime.

You can volunteer your time to help people learn to read through literacy or tutoring programs. Reading Is Fundamental is a national organization that may have a local chapter in your hometown.

Animals

According to Friends of Animals, animal shelters in the United States euthanize more than 18 million dogs and cats every year, many of whom have been abused and abandoned by their owners. Statistics about animals in the wild are just as discouraging: Entire species are on the brink of extinction. The U.S. Fish and Wildlife Service reports that blue whales, timber wolves, tigers, leopards, and California condors are all endangered.

Many people feel passionate about helping and protecting animals. Do you enjoy spending time with cats, dogs, and other pets? If so, volunteering with animals might be very rewarding for you. Look in the phone book for animal shelters or your local Society for the Prevention of Cruelty to Animals (SPCA). You can help by walking dogs or playing with cats so that they

If you love animals, you can volunteer to help at a local animal shelter or SPCA.

get exercise and do not grow up afraid of people. You can help clean the cages and feed the animals. Some places even have rescue organizations that go out and rescue abandoned pets from the streets, clean them up, and find homes for them.

Political Campaigns

If it's an election year, either locally or nationally, there will be lots of opportunities for volunteer work at many different levels. You could do anything from answering phones and licking envelopes to campaigning door-to-door and organizing rallies. Political campaigns can be good short-term, intense experiences in which you learn firsthand the ins and outs of the election process. In addition, you will meet a lot of people who are influential in your community.

Disaster Aid

Every year thousands of Americans are victims of disasters like home fires, tornadoes, floods, and hurricanes. The Red Cross is a national organization that provides relief to a lot of families in need of temporary emergency assistance, including food and shelter, medical care, and blood donations. The Red Cross always needs volunteers, especially during disasters.

There are hundreds, if not thousands of worthwhile charitable causes. This is just a partial list of issues that might inspire you to get involved. Most of these ideas are ways for you to join already-existing organizations or projects. But there is nothing to stop you from starting your own volunteer project.

Chapter Three

Find Your Passion

You have the power to make good things happen in this world. With passion, enthusiasm, and focused energy, you can make a difference. That is one of the great joys of volunteering: learning how wonderful it feels to make a positive impact on the world and people around you. If you are ready to get started with volunteering, then it's time to think through some important questions.

- What means a lot to me?
- What needs to be changed?
- What skills do I have?
- What are my strengths and weaknesses?
- What kind of work do I want to do?
- Do I like to work indoors or outdoors?
- Would I rather work for an organization or design a project of my own?

- Would I rather work by myself or with a group of people?

- Do I like to work directly with those in need or am I better at organizing and administration?

These are good questions for you to think about and discuss with someone you respect, like a school guidance counselor or your parents, who can give you good advice. You may even want to write down the answers in a journal or notebook.

Choosing the Volunteer Job Best Suited for You

You need to think carefully about the issues you care about and the kinds of work that appeal to you before making a commitment to a project or to an organization. A commitment is just that—you are agreeing to be somewhere and do something and people will depend on you to keep your word. You must treat it like a real job. Even though you are not getting paid, people are relying on you to complete your work.

When you choose a project that you care deeply about, you'll be rewarded and satisfied with your volunteer experience. Loving what you do is also a great way to stay motivated to continue your work, even when you get busy. You can use the interest inventory on the following pages to help you finalize your decisions about where and how to focus your volunteer efforts.

Making a list of your interests can help you determine where to devote your time and energy.

Interest Inventory: An Assessment

This inventory is meant to help you decide where to devote your time and energy. It is a starting point, especially if you feel overwhelmed by the many choices and the many needs. Fill it out as honestly as you can. Think hard about what you like as opposed to what you think might be the popular choice or what your friends would choose. Volunteering is not only for those whom you are benefiting, it is a great way for you to grow and learn and understand the world around you. Finding "your" cause can be a really important part of your development as you move into adulthood. Let's try to narrow down your interests to give you a jumping-off point for your volunteer work.

"I get excited about . . ."

For each "I get excited about . . ." list, put a "1" by the activities you like most, a "2" by your second favorite choices, and a "3" by your third choices.

1. I get excited about . . .

   a. Helping board up an abandoned house

   b. Starting a canned food drive at school for donations to a food pantry

   c. Planning a walk-a-thon to raise money for breast cancer research

   d. Planning a party for the children's ward at a local hospital

   e. Planning a community garden and planting trees

   f. Serving as a tour guide at the art museum

   g. Making flashcards of words for people who are learning to read

   h. Speaking out about the importance of spaying or neutering pets

   i. Hanging up posters and handing out leaflets for a candidate before an election

   j. Collecting donations for earthquake victims in another country

2. I get excited about . . .

   a. Collecting toiletries (toothbrushes, tooth paste, soap) for homeless people

b. Preparing food baskets for needy families

c. Collecting old eyeglasses and donating them to the Lion's Club for needy children

d. Conducting an arts and crafts activity at a preschool

e. Working on building and maintaining the trails in a park

f. Taking tickets at the symphony

g. Reading to children in after-school programs

h. Helping rescue abandoned cats from alleys

i. Helping register people to vote at a local fair

j. Collecting blankets and canned goods for flood victims

3. I get excited about . . .

a. Working with Habitat for Humanity on a house-building project

b. Preparing and serving lunch at a soup kitchen

c. Working at a health booth at a street festival to promote wellness

d. Organizing a youth olympics for the children in my neighborhood or at my church or temple

e. Starting a recycling campaign in my neighborhood

f. Working as an usher at a theater

Reading to children in an after-school program may be exciting and rewarding for you.

g. Working on reshelving books at the library

h. Walking dogs at the local animal shelter

i. Making phone calls for a mayoral candidate

j. Helping organize a blood drive

Each response begins with a letter of the alphabet. For each response you marked with a 1, 2, or 3, write its letter here. For example, 1: c, f, j, c, f.

1:

2:

3:

Would you rather . . .

Just as you did with the previous lists, mark each "Would you rather . ." list with a "1" by the activities you like most, a "2" by your second favorite choices, and a "3" by your third choices.

1. Would you rather . . .

   a. Answer phones and file papers

   b. Write a grant

   c. Read stories to groups of children at the local library

   d. Make posters for a benefit auction

   e. Complete a walk-a-thon

   f. Address the Rotary Club about a particular cause or organization

2. Would you rather . . .

   a. Work on a big mailing for an organization

   b. Participate in a phone-a-thon, making phone calls to strangers to raise money

   c. Visit people in a local nursing home during the holidays

   d. Clean up a local park

   e. Go door-to-door in your neighborhood, encouraging people to vote

   f. Visit a local radio station to talk about an important cause

3. Would you rather . . .

   a. Write materials to publicize an issue or an organization

b. Work with businesses in your neighborhood to collect spare change from customers for a good cause

c. Serve lunch at a homeless shelter

d. Be on a committee to plan a fund-raising dinner and dance

e. Help paint a local elementary school

f. Make a speech in a school assembly

Each response begins with a letter of the alphabet. For each response you marked with a 1, 2, or 3, write its letter here. For example, 1: a, d, e, a.

1:

2:

3:

Interpreting your results

In the "I get excited about..." section (the first three lists), the same letter represents the same issue category. Here are the issue categories:

a. homelessness and shelter

b. hunger and poverty

c. health

d. children

e. nature and the environment

f. arts and culture

g. literacy

h. animals

i. politics

j. disaster aid

In the "Would you rather . . ." section (the second three lists), the letters represent the same category of volunteer activities. Here are the activity categories:

a. provide administrative support

b. raise funds

c. work directly with people

d. organize or plan events

e. participate in an activity

f. promote an organization or cause

Look back at how you scored this inventory. Your first choices (anything you scored with a 1) are your strongest areas of interest. If two or more of your first choices are the same letter, that indicates a very strong interest in that particular issue or activity. If you have scored a particular letter with a 3, that means you don't have much of an interest in that issue/activity or you need to learn more about that issue/activity before you commit to a volunteer project.

How Much Time Do You Have?

You can volunteer after school or on the weekends. You can volunteer during the summer or over school holidays. Most teens volunteer a few hours a week or a few days a month. You have to decide how much time you have and the most important thing is to be realistic. The number one complaint supervisors have about volunteers is that they promise to come at a certain time and then don't show up.

Consider the classes you are taking, how much homework you have, family commitments, chores, and other activities that might interfere with your volunteer schedule (like if you play on a sports team or take music lessons).

Some volunteer jobs have flexible times and others are more structured. If you are crunched for time, you might consider a one-time volunteer activity, such as donating clothes to the Salvation Army, collecting money for UNICEF at Halloween, or bringing canned goods to a food pantry. These one-time activities might be a good way to start your volunteer efforts to see what you really enjoy. Sometimes, you never know until you try.

You can find a list of local nonprofit organizations in your public library.

Chapter Four

Getting Started

Now that you have an issue in mind, it's time to find a place to do your volunteer work. Two good starting points are your local phone book and the central branch of your local library. Check your yellow pages for organizations that deal with your chosen issue. In your library, work with a librarian to see if there are community resource books that provide information about the kinds of nonprofit organizations in your hometown. If you can locate a resource guide, look for descriptions of work or projects that interest you, as well as contact information for the organization. You will want to speak to the executive director or the volunteer coordinator.

Make a list of possible organizations, with telephone numbers and addresses for each.

Applying for a Volunteer Job

Applying for a volunteer job is not really any different from applying for a paid job. You should take this process seriously and act professionally.

The first contact will be up to you, so get out that list you made and find a quiet place where you can use the telephone. Call your chosen organization and tell the person who answers that you are calling because you are interested in volunteering. Be sure to state your name clearly. Find out whom you should speak to about volunteer opportunities. He or she may not be available to speak with you at that time, so you may have to leave a message. Make sure you give all your information (name, phone number) and make sure that you write down your contact person's name, in case you need to call back. Thank the person who answered the phone for taking your message.

Wait for a few days and see if you get a call back. If not, try calling the person again. Your persistence will show that you are serious in your desire to volunteer, but don't call every day. The person you need to speak to may be very busy or may be out of the office for a few days. Be patient and polite.

Writing a letter is another way to approach the situation. First, call the organization and find out to whom you should address the letter. Make sure to get the correct spelling of his or her name. It goes without saying

You should apply for a volunteer job as you would apply for a paid position.

that your letter should be neat and edited carefully for proper grammar and spelling. It is preferable that your letter be typed. In the letter explain that you are interested in volunteer work. Include your name, address, and phone number. You might include a self-addressed, stamped envelope for the organization's use in sending you materials or information.

Some organizations will require you to fill out an application. They may mail the application to you and expect you to send it back to them completed. They may set up an interview with you and ask you to fill out the application at that time. You will need to write neatly and clearly. Most applications will ask you questions about your experience, your school grades, hobbies, and interests. Do the best that you can and ask questions about anything you don't understand. You may not have prior job experience, but think about similar or related "work" you may have done at your church or in your school. Be sure to highlight all accomplishments, awards, or honors.

Some applications will ask you why you want to volunteer or what interests you in this particular organization. It will be helpful to think of the answer to these questions in advance so that you are prepared.

Interviewing for a Volunteer Job

Once an organization decides it is interested in having you as a volunteer, you may be asked to come in for an interview. Depending on the organization, this may be a formal interview or an informal meeting. It's best to be prepared for a formal situation, which means dressing nicely and looking your best. You want to make a good first impression and you want to convey that you think this job is important.

Arrive at your interview a few minutes early, in case there is any paperwork you have to fill out. The interview will likely focus on the organization and its work (for your information) and questions about you (for the interviewer's information). The interviewer will probably ask you about your experience and your interests. Once the interviewer has asked you his or her questions, you should feel free to ask questions of your own. You might want to consider questions such as the following:

You may be asked to interview for a volunteer job. Be polite and make sure to ask questions about the organization.

- How many volunteers work for this organization and what kind of things do they work on?
- How long do volunteers generally stay with this organization?
- How old are the other volunteers I would be working with?
- How much experience do the other volunteers have?
- Who supervises the volunteers?
- What kind of training or orientation is provided for volunteers?

When the interview is over, shake the interviewer's hand and thank the person for his or her time. When you get home, take the time to write a thank-you note to the person who interviewed you. This small gesture shows your professional attitude and your maturity, and says a lot about the kind of volunteer you will be.

You Got the Job!

Getting "hired" for a volunteer job is a big accomplishment—congratulations! Now you can start making your contribution. That means that you need to show up on specific days at a specific time and complete the tasks assigned to you. If you are sick or for some reason you can't make it in, you need to call and let the organization know you won't be there.

Find out who your boss or supervisor will be. It is very important to listen to your supervisor and follow his or her instructions. Show the person respect and you can expect he or she will show the same respect to you.

You will probably make new friends at your volunteer job. Resist the temptation to joke around or chat too much. This is a job. You have chosen an important issue and now is your time to make a difference. Save the socializing for after work. Remember that you might need a good review from your supervisor for school credit. You might want to ask your supervisor to be a reference when you apply to a job in the future, or even for a college application. Regardless, you came to do a job and that should be your top priority.

Chapter Five

Do It Yourself!

If you are convinced that going out on your own is the best way to volunteer your time, then use the following guidelines to get your project up and running. Some of the first things to think about are the same as for any kind of volunteering (like making a decision about what issues you plan to address), but they are even more important when starting from scratch. There will be additional challenges to starting a project of your own, so don't enter into this lightly. But there will also be the satisfaction of knowing you did it on your own.

Research Your Project

After you have chosen your issue and you have come up with an idea for a project, here are some questions to ask yourself:

- How does this issue affect my community?

- Who or what is most affected and thus would benefit most from a volunteer project?

- What can I do that would make the biggest contribution?

- What would I like to do?

- What can I do?

- How much time do I have to devote to this project?

- What else do I need to know before I get started?

- Who can help me?

Form a Team

Maybe you need more people to help you accomplish your goal or maybe you aren't comfortable working alone and want to recruit some others to join you. Choose people who share your interest and who are committed to completing the project (you don't want to be left holding the bag halfway through). Consider your friends, family members, and people at your school, church, clubs, or in your neighborhood as possible teammates. You don't have to limit your team to people your own age. You might benefit from inviting younger kids to participate or maybe you need an adult to help.

A team of committed people can help you complete your volunteer project.

Find a Sponsor

Sponsors help you by providing anything from money to guidance to supplies that you will need. Also, being affiliated with a person or organization that is respected in the community can lend credibility to your cause. Think about whether a sponsor would help you meet your goals. If you do work with a sponsor, make sure you have a clear agreement about what the sponsor will provide and what the sponsor expects of you.

It is very important to remember that when you take on a sponsor, you are an extension of that organization. If it is an individual person who is your sponsor, the actions of your group have an impact on that person's reputation. You have a responsibility to

Setting a schedule is an important step toward achieving your goals.

the person to act professionally, follow through on your commitments, and always speak positively and supportively about your sponsor.

Make a Plan

You will need to make some decisions about the project, such as:

- When and where will you meet? You need to meet frequently enough to get the work done and keep people connected but not so frequently that your team gets burned out.

- How will you get to your meeting place?

- What is your goal? What do you want to accomplish?

◆ Set a schedule. How long will the project take? What needs to be done first? Set deadlines to accomplish specific tasks. How much time will each step take? When will you be finished?

◆ Estimate your costs. What do you need to get started? What will you need along the way? Anticipate any costs and plan for them up front. Think about transportation, supplies, equipment, postage, photocopying. What else? Keep in mind that local stores will often donate or discount goods or services if you let them know that it is for a charitable cause. It never hurts to ask.

◆ Assign tasks. Who will be responsible for what? How will you communicate with each other about your work?

◆ Think through your plan carefully—is anything missing? Is it too complicated? Do you need to make any changes? Does everyone on your team agree with the plan?

Consider Your Target Audience

Make sure that the people or group you want to serve actually wants or needs your service. You need to make sure that the issue you think of as a problem is really considered a problem by the people involved. (This can be a sensitive situation. For example, if you want to help some elderly people in your church with their yard work, you need to make sure that they want your help and that they won't be offended by your suggestions.) This can be accomplished by meeting with the people, sending them a letter, or placing a phone call and asking for their reaction to your idea.

Talk to them about their needs. If they are different than you think, you might need to revise your plan.

Decide Where to Perform the Service

- ◆ Will you go to the project or the people or will they come to you?

- ◆ Where will your service be performed or your project carried out?

- ◆ Do you have any special space requirements (for example, if you are collecting canned goods, do you have a place to store them)?

If you will be working in someone else's space (like a school or community center), visit the space first to make sure it has everything you will need. If it doesn't, what do you need to bring?

Publicize Your Issue and Your Project

How will you let others know about your project? What do you want to communicate about your project? What kind of attention do you want?

Posting fliers is a great way to publicize your project.

There are many means of communication available to you. Do you want to tell people in your neighborhood about an environmental problem? Making fliers and putting them at people's doors or posting them in local stores is a good way to publicize your issue. If you have a community-wide issue and you need to reach a lot of people at once, look into public service announcements on the local television and radio stations. You can also write a press release for your local newspaper; it may write a story about your group.

Raise Any Needed Funds

Do you need startup money, special equipment, or supplies to accomplish your project?

If your project will cost you anything besides pocket money, you have to think through a budget (what you need and how much it will cost) and a plan to raise the money. Fund-raisers take a lot of preplanning. There are lots of books in the library with ideas about how to raise money. Sometimes there are small grants available for youth to work on community projects. Talk to a teacher or a librarian for more help. There may be people at your church with fund-raising experience as well.

Evaluate Your Project When It's Over

Think about your experience. Discuss the project with your teammates and with the people you served (if appropriate) or write about it in a journal. Whether you are planning to repeat the service or move on to something else, you need to know what you learned and what you accomplished. Don't be afraid to admit that you made mistakes or that there were aspects that need improvement.

Think about questions like:

- What did I learn?
- What did I accomplish?
- How do I feel about the project?
- Would I do it again?
- How could I improve it?

Chapter Six

Volunteering as a Way of Life

Volunteering can be contagious. What might start as a volunteer project after school could become a consuming passion and then a way of life. You might decide to make your volunteer passion into a profession. As you get older, there will be opportunities for you to continue and expand your volunteer work.

What I Did over My Summer Vacation

As you grow and develop your volunteering skills and your interest in a particular issue, you may wish to devote more time to your cause. Summer vacations are a great time to volunteer. If you have already been volunteering, summer is a chance to intensify your experience. You might consider volunteering full-time during the summer or joining a program that takes you away from home for a summer of volunteer work.

There are lots of great options. Some towns have youth employment programs that allow you to do good work in your own community and earn a little money. Some organizations run big volunteer efforts during the summer that you can join. For example, Habitat for Humanity does most of its house building in the United States during the summer. You can join them for a day, a week, or a month-long building blitz. If you want to travel and learn a foreign language, consider researching a program for volunteering abroad.

Volunteer around the World

Volunteer work can take you all over the world. There are many worthwhile causes in other countries all around the globe. Check your local library or on-line for information about organizations that sponsor short trips or extended stays in other countries for volunteers. Check whether programs require special skills or language proficiency. You will find that there are opportunities to spend a week, a summer, or two years working as a volunteer in numerous countries on a variety of issues from education to agriculture and the environment.

Sometimes these programs cost money, especially if airfare is required. Don't be discouraged by the cost

Volunteer projects can lead to travel opportunities, like this Volunteers for Peace work-study program in Estonia.

of volunteering. If you can't afford the fees required to participate in your project of choice, contact the sponsoring organization and ask if it provides financial sponsorship, assistance with fund-raising, or grants. Sometimes religious institutions will help with fund-raising efforts or contribute funds toward a volunteer trip.

Summer Programs to Consider

Amigos de las Américas
5618 Star Lane
Houston, TX 77057
(800) 231-7796
Web site: http://www.amigoslink.org

American Jewish Society for Service
15 East 26th Street, Room 1029
New York, NY 10010
(212) 683-6178
Web site: http://www.ajss.org

Volunteers for Peace
1034 Tiffany Road
Belmont, VT 05730-0202
(802) 259-2759
Web site: http://www.vfp.org

After High School

When you finish high school, you may decide you are not ready to enter college right away. Or you might need to earn some money to pay for college. Volunteering is a possible way to use your time, gain some experience, and even earn money toward an education, with the added bonus of working on important and interesting projects.

In 1994, President Clinton started a national program called Americorps. Young people eighteen years and older can sign up to do community service for up to two years. Some programs even allow you to extend your commitment for a third year. You can choose an Americorps program based on where you want to live to do this service, what issue you want to work on, or both. There are nearly 1,000 national and local groups that participate with Americorps.

In return, you receive a modest living stipend plus an educational award. If you work full-time, you will receive $4,725 for every year of service you complete. Part-time work will earn you a portion of that award. This award can be used to finance college, pay off existing college loans, or pay for graduate school. There are hundreds of programs to choose from, all over the United States.

The Power of You

Are you convinced of your power and the power of teens everywhere? Are you ready to save the world? The advantages of your youth are many: You have the energy, commitment, freedom, passion, and belief that change can happen. Your simple actions can set off a chain of events that starts by touching individual lives and finishes by shaping the future.

Careful thinking and planning combined with the power of you will result in an unstoppable force for kindness, justice, peace, and humanity. You have an incredible opportunity and a serious responsibility in this life. It's up to you to take the difficult first step. Once started, you—and the world—will never be the same.

Glossary

Americorps The national community service program that pays young people a small living stipend and an educational award for each year of service completed.

cause An issue, problem, situation, or value that people care about, raise money for, work on, or support.

chapter A branch of an organization.

compassion Sympathy for the hardship of others and a desire to help.

docent A person who leads guided tours in a museum or art gallery.

euthanize The act of killing a hopelessly ill or injured individual or animal in a merciful, painless way.

evaluate To determine the importance or worth of something through careful study.

fund To give money to support a cause or an organization.

fund-raising The organized activity of raising money for an institution or a cause.

illiteracy The inability to read or write.

nonprofit organization   An organization that conducts its activity or business without making a financial profit and has special tax status with the federal government.

press release   A publicity tool that gives information to newspapers, radio and television stations, and other media outlets.

publicity   An act or tool used to gain public interest, support, or attention; advertising.

recruit   To invite people to join an activity or organization.

reference   A person familiar with your character or your work experience who can vouch for you or make a statement about you when you are applying for a job or to an educational institution.

sponsor   A person or organization that provides funds, guidance, or assistance to complete a project or carry out an activity.

volunteer   A person who performs a service without financial or legal gain.

Where to Go for Help

In the United States

Corporation for National Service
1201 New York Avenue, NW
Washington, DC 20525
(202) 606-5000
Web site: http://www.americorps.org

Points of Light Foundation
1400 I Street NW, Suite 800
Washington, DC 20005
(800) 879-5400
Web site: http://www.pointsoflight.org

Youth Service America
1101 15th Street, Suite 200
Washington, DC 20005
(202) 296-2992
Web site: http://www.servenet.org

In Canada

Volunteer Canada
430 Gilmour Street
Ottawa, ON K2P 0R8
(800) 670-0401

The Youth Resource Network of Canada
Web site: http: //www. youth.gc.ca

Web Resources

http://www.areyouintoit.com
This is 4-H's Web site about volunteering.

http://www.geocities.com/volguide
On-line volunteer guide, targeted primarily at youth in Palm
Beach County, Florida. However, it contains great general
information, as well as links to all the volunteer opportunity
search engines.

http://www.kidscare.org
Kids Care Clubs are clubs started by young people interested in
volunteer service. This site tells you how to start a club and
provides a lot of information about volunteering.

http://www.pitchin.org
An e-zine that celebrates youth volunteer service.

Volunteer Opportunity Search Engines
http://americaspromise.org
List of volunteer programs in the United States.

http://www.idealist.org
Lists over 20,000 organizations in 140 countries.

http://volunteermatch.org
Has made over 150,000 volunteer matches.

For Further Reading

Duper, Linda Leeb. *160 Ways to Help the World: Community Service Projects for Young People.* New York: Facts on File, 1996.

Lewis, Barbara A. *The Kid's Guide to Service Projects: Over 500 Service Ideas for Young People Who Want to Make a Difference.* Minneapolis, MN: Free Spirit Publishing, Inc., 1995.

———. *The Kid's Guide to Social Action.* Minneapolis. MN: Free Spirit Publishing, Inc., 1998.

———. *What Do You Stand For? A Kid's Guide to Building Character.* Minneapolis, MN: Free Spirit Publishing, Inc., 1997.

Ryan, Bernard. *Community Service for Teens.* Chicago: Ferguson Publishing Company, 1998.

Salzman, Marian, and Teresa Reisgies. *150 Ways Teens Can Make a Difference.* Princeton, NJ: Peterson's, 1991.

Index

Acknowledgments

Thanks to my wonderful husband, Doug Fireside, my family, and my friends for their continued support and encouragement. Special thanks to Erika McClammy, Heidi Paremske, and Lisa Smith for your help with this book and also for the important—and often unrecognized—work you do for Baltimore.

About the Author

Laura Weeldreyer works on public school reform in Baltimore, Maryland. She is the author of *Body Blues: The Link Between Weight and Depression* and *Cha Ching! The Girl's Guide to Saving Money*. Ms. Weeldreyer has been and continues to be an active, passionate volunteer—especially on issues that affect children and young people.

Photo Credits

Cover and pp. 8, 30, 38, 41, 43, 47, 48, 51 by Darren Turner; p. 2 © FPG International; p. 12 © Steven Skjold; pp. 16, 26, 33 by Thaddeus Harden; p. 20 © Pictor; p. 23 © Shaun Walker/AP/Worldwide; p. 55 © Volunteers for Peace.

Layout

Geri Giordano

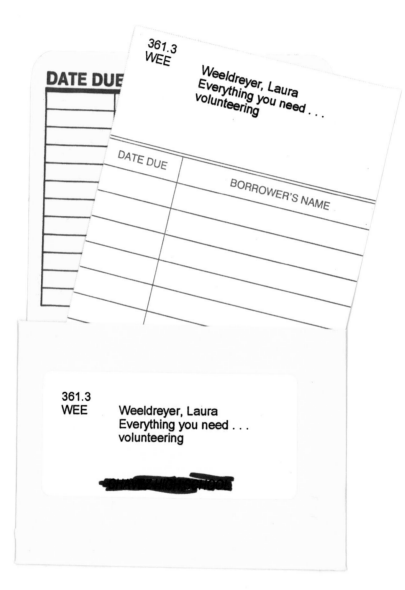

DATE DUE

361.3
WEE

Weeldreyer, Laura
Everything you need . . .
volunteering

DATE DUE

BORROWER'S NAME